MY FUTURE IS BRIGHT LIKE SUNSHINE

AFFIRMATION COLORING BOOK

_____

_____

_____

Daily sayings to promote confidence, love and self esteem

Believe in yourself!

I AM HELPFUL

I BELIEVE MY FUTURE IS BRIGHT LIKE SUNSHINE

I AM GREATFUL FOR WHAT I HAVE

You are completely and unconditionally loved!

I LOVE TO LEARN NEW THINGS

Don't forget to be awesome!

I AM BLESED BEYOND MEASURE

I AM HAPPY

Be kind to others but also be kind to yourself!

I LEARN FAST

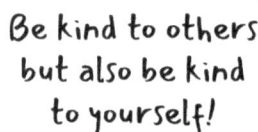

I AM LOVED

Asking for help shows your strength and courage!

I HAVE AMAZING ABILITIES

I AM VALUED AND IMPORTANT